# GRACED
## FOR IMPACT
## A Memoir

By:
Tequila Michelle

© 2020 by Tequila Michelle

Graced for Impact - A Memoir

Printed in the United States of America

ISBN: 978-0-578-73646-4

Cover by Armor of Hope Writing & Publishing Services

Edited by Armor of Hope Writing & Publishing Services

# CONTENTS

# ACKNOWLEDGEMENTS

I would like to thank God for giving me the strength to tell my story and to the Holy Spirit, the comforter, for guiding me through this process. It has been a long and treacherous journey. However, I never gave up. It has taken me years to become the person I am today. I pray that my story helps you exercise your faith, in hope of bringing healing and closure to your inner man. I believe that no one can tell your story better than you, so tell your story and take back the power the enemy has stolen!

I would like to thank my spiritual leadership: Apostle Cary Rashad, Apostle Valinda Fuquay-Mack, Prophet Cedric Moses, and Pastor Darron Massey. You all are dear to my heart. Each of you had a role in my Christian walk. I do not take the role you played for granted. I am thankful that I've had the pleasure of knowing each of you. When I wanted to stray, you didn't let me. When I wanted to give up, you guided me. When things got blurry, you hid me within your arms. For all those acts of kindness, I will never forget you. Thank you for instilling values, morals, ethics, and most importantly the Word deep within my heart! I am forever grateful.

To my mom and dad, I wouldn't be here without you two. I would like to sincerely thank you for all of your sacrifices. You two raised me to be a talented, inspiring, and smart woman. All of the lessons I had to learn from your successes and mistakes allowed me to become a well-rounded person. For that, I will make sure you two are taken care of in your latter years.

To my mentors Rachelle McMillan and Moni B., you both have inspired me to become a better person. You have done this with your courses and advice. I would have never known the power that lay dormant in me. I am forever grateful for you both for taking me under your wings and showing me the ropes! Thank you.

To Quandra Adams, you have been there for me since the beginning of time. Starting from our college dorms to now owning several businesses, we have watched each other grow exponentially. I speak blessings upon your life and businesses as you have taught me that no matter how you grew up or the circumstances that may arise, I too can rise above it! Your tenacity, diligence, and professionalism meant the world to me. Thank you!

To my future husband, someday you will read this book and know you were sent to me. I pray you understand who I was then and who I am now. All I ask is that you love me like Christ loved the Church, with every fiber of your being. Most importantly, I would love to partner with you in life! I know that we both would be tailored for one another, and I am ecstatic to see what's in store. I pray I am everything and more in which you sought our Father God for. In Jesus Christ's name, Amen.

# PREFACE

While on this journey, I learned something very important. I found there is a difference between honesty and transparency. Honesty is a weak characteristic in my opinion. Why? Because people are only honest when probed by a question, and only then do they decide to tell the truth. However, a person who's transparent doesn't need a question to be asked to speak their truth. They simply tell the truth regardless. So, I ask, which of these characteristics do you have?

# INTRODUCTION

---

Where do I start?  It is my hope that this book may heal you, deliver you, and help grow your faith. I am not looking to be honest in this book, but transparent. Speaking my truth to help someone in need is all that I ask. I want to use my testimony to set people free! Buckle your seat belts and let's ride!

"Now we who are strong ought to bear the weaknesses of those without strength and not just please ourselves" (Romans 15:1 NASB).

# CHAPTER 1
## BACK IN THE DAY

Listening to the song *Back in the Day* by Ahmad brought back some good (and bad) memories from my childhood. I didn't have a bad childhood necessarily, but I didn't remember many things as a kid. If I think back, there were probably circumstances I wished would've been different. I am the only child of both parents, who are still living. I thank God I still have them in my life, no matter how I feel about my upbringing. My mom was a single parent because my dad left her when I was only six months old. At least, that was her side of the story. My dad, on the other hand, said she cheated on him and that's why he left. Either way, that's no excuse as to why he wasn't there. I get it. Sometimes a mother becomes bitter and angry because of the father's neglect. As a result, the dad may be forced to stay away. I may never get the entire truth of what happened, but it doesn't matter because what is done is done. I have forgiven them both for their neglect of me, directly or indirectly.

That being said, I didn't grow up with the luxury of living in a two-parent household as many other kids. My mom always worked to provide for me as much as she could, so I hardly have memories of spending time with her. My dad was in and out of jail and was what I like to call a *street pharmacist*. Mom would always call him a *deadbeat dad*, and I didn't understand why. I don't know why folks think because a parent doesn't give monetarily, that's what makes them a deadbeat. There may be other factors at play. However, in reality, a child truly values the time spent, not money. A kid would rather be in their parents' presence. It doesn't matter if they get the latest shoes, clothes, or gadgets. A parent emotionally investing in and spending time with their child is all they want or need, at least that was the case for me.

My mom was (and still is) bitter about that situation. I can tell. There would be times that she and I would get into an argument because I wouldn't give her my dad's address for the sake of receiving child support. The next thing from her would be, "You're just like your daddy!" Those words were detrimental to my spirit. Hearing them made me cringe. They made me angry and resentful towards her. How could she compare my character to what he had done? Their relationship shaped my idea of what love was supposed to look like. I don't think my mom knew what love was either. My grandmother, her mother, had eight kids. How can a person possibly devote all their time, attention, care, and love equally without some of the children falling through the cracks? It's an arduous task that's exhausting for anybody. All I'm saying is somebody didn't get what they were supposed to. As a result, some were neglected. I can hardly remember the last time my mother said, "I love you" to me. I only have one photo of us with her holding me in her arms as an infant. It should be a given that a mother shows affection for her children; it seems like common sense. But I realized her relationship and attitude toward me may have stemmed from what she experienced in her own childhood.

You know, growing up in a black household isn't easy. As children, we are forced to become adults way before our time. We had responsibilities like doing extra chores, paying bills, and watching our siblings. Some of us were even *latch-key* kids. If you remember having a key tied to a shoestring, you were a *latch-key* kid. I can remember being a *latch-key* kid around nine or ten years old. My mother would tie a key to an old shoestring and either hang it around my neck or put it in my bookbag. When I got home, I knew exactly what to do. My mom would instruct me to close the door and answer the phone when she called. Not to mention, she demanded I never answer the door! It's a sad reality for most black children; we have to do what we have to do in order to survive.

Now, let's fast forward. I graduated from Southern High School in Durham, North Carolina. I was in the class of 2004. I wasn't at the top of my class, but I did reasonably well for myself, considering the cards I was dealt. I was very active in after school activities. I played the flute in the wind ensemble band. I was a majorette/flag girl in the marching band, and was a part of the medical program, graduating with my certified nursing assistant license. I didn't grow up in the suburbs or anything, but what I call the *hood,* where watching people get shot and stabbed was the norm. I was no saint. Watching all of those things go on, I was smoking by the time I was fourteen. I thought I was grown, smoking those WAVE cigarettes with a friend of mine at the time. I also got involved with a boy who was my first love. No, not in the way you might be thinking. I became consumed with him. I stayed out late, skipped school, and even tried to join a gang to be close to him. He was a part of the *Bloods*. Some of my neighborhood girlfriends and I decided we would form a gang of our own called *B.T.O*, short for *B*****s Taking Over*. We rocked the American Flag paraphernalia. From Chuck Taylor shoes, du-rags, hell...anything we could find, we made it our thing. We even had a handshake! We were serious about it too. As I grew closer to this guy, my mother began noticing I was acting different. My wardrobe consisted of red and black because I felt it was a way to get closer to him. Then, I looked up one day, and he was gone. I found out through some of his blood brothers his mom sent him away to New York City, his hometown. I can still remember the day he left; he looked back out the car window, never to return. I was completely devastated. So, I buried all the hate and hurt I was feeling, ruminating in it instead of releasing it. I believe that was the beginning of my unforgiving heart. From that moment, my life changed. I began to be *Bitter Betty*.

Through all of this, my mother found out that I was smoking. By that point, it had escalated from smoking cigarettes to smoking *Mary Jane*, also known as weed or marijuana. I loved it, and it became a part of my daily life. I remember like it was yesterday, when my mom found out. I came into the house, forgetting I had just rolled two blunts, and I stuck them in my front pockets. Mom noticed them and yanked them from me so quick that I didn't have time for a reaction. My mom broke them in half and asked, "What is this? Are you smoking now, Quila?" I replied, "Yes." She was furious and disappointed at the same time. I could see it all in her disposition. She told me she was going to tell my dad. I'm not gonna lie. I was terrified of my dad. The streets knew my dad as *Dolla.* So, when he got wind of me smoking, he called a meeting with me. I went with him for a weekend, and I just knew I was going to get the whooping of my life! I was ready for the consequences. My dad took me to the store and bought a five pack of Dutch Masters, the blue pack to be exact. He said, "Since you want to be grown and do grown-up things, I am going to teach you a lesson." He instructed me to take a bath, and when I came out, he had everything laid out for me. He told me to roll every blunt full of weed. I swear it was at least 7.5 grams. Then he said, "Now smoke every last blunt by yourself." My eyes lit up. *Is he for real?* Sure enough, it was real. I was lit (as the young folks would say)! Little did he know, he turned me into a straight pothead. For most kids, this act of punishment would have been enough to straighten up but not Tequila. I loved smoking weed. It became embedded in my blood. There was no stopping me. They had created a monster. What did they expect? I mean, my mom was a weed and hash smoker back then, and my dad was a street pharmacist. Did they not think they would create a hybrid of themselves or that their actions would not influence me in some way eventually? From that point forward, my view was skewed.

While all the girls in the neighborhood were chasing down the most popular guys, I was too busy trying to get high, but I had a whole lot of restrictions. I had to come in when the streetlights came on, couldn't go to any parties, and if I did, I had to come in at a particular time. I felt like a caged bird. I thank God for the turnaround though. At some point, I began to realize I needed to get my act straight before graduating. I set goals for myself. I didn't have sex until I turned eighteen, which I thought was responsible at the time.  Then, I met a guy, who we'll call *Light Bright*. He was my everything. Extremely sweet, he played the piano and loved sports. He was a gentleman. I met him in twelfth grade; he was a freshman at NCCU. He often snuck into my dorm room and spent the night at Baynes Hall. That's right! I attended North Carolina Central University. EAGLE PRIDE! I thought he was the one I would marry.

Little did he know, I wasn't who he thought I was. He later found out I smoked, was a partygoer, and I drank liquor. I used to take baths before going to see him because I thought he wouldn't be able to smell the smoke on me but he did. A non-smoker can *always* smell smoke. He confronted me about it. It turned him off of course, and he later broke up with me because of it. My life flashed before my eyes. I truly loved him, and I thought my world was over.

About two weeks had passed, and I noticed my body was acting funny. Time had passed since I had sex with him, but the reminder of it immediately sent me into panic. I went to the hospital, and they ran all kinds of tests. For one, I had a really bad UTI and didn't know. It was to the point they had to flush my kidneys, and I had to stay in the hospital for days! They couldn't figure out what was wrong. The last resort was to take a blood test and do a STD culture exam. Lord, have mercy! It was so nerve-wracking. My test came back positive for an STD. To think that someone I loved caused this, my heart was crushed! For all intents and purposes, I made sure to take every precaution and be safe, so I was shocked that this still happened despite my preparation.

After a few weeks of gathering my thoughts and emotions, I called my ex, *Light Bright*, to discuss what had happened. Of course, I got the typical male response. He claimed he didn't know, but I kept praying for answers because I knew it was a lie, at least that's how he spun it. After a while, he confessed. When he visited home during school break, he had sex with an ex-girlfriend. That was his way of telling me he cheated to justify what happened to me. That confession told me everything I needed to know. So, from my father to *Brooklyn*, then to my college boyfriend, I realized a pattern was forming. I recognized I didn't have a good record of successful male relationships because my dad was almost never there to show me what love was supposed to look like and how a man should treat me. A girl's father is her first love. He is supposed to set the example.

To deal with all of this, I bottled it up inside and swept it under the rug. It seemed I wasn't going to get the answers I deserved, so I went on about my life. The repercussions from that had a detrimental effect on my desire to seek a healthy relationship. I closed my heart off to the thought of falling in love. I started going to parties, drinking and smoking more weed than usual. I did all the things that a caged bird would do upon its release. I began to experience a lot of things. From that point, I didn't entertain many guys. My self-esteem was shot. I couldn't come to terms with what he did. It left me heartbroken, regretful, and distrustful. But I guess that's just a part of the game. My scenario is just one example of why you shouldn't have premarital sex!

Fast forward about a year later. I met another guy. I'm going to call him *Mr. M.I.A.* He was definitely an alpha-male. He had his own place, cars, dogs, was a club promoter...you name it, he had it. He treated me well for a time. After a while, though, I noticed some things were off. I was thinking I was the only one he was dealing with, but nope! He had multiple *friends*. So, you know, I was one of his cut buddies. However, I had no problem with it because he wasn't my man. We weren't exclusive. He was the possessive type though. When he wanted something, he got it. Oh, but it was something about the Caribbean influence! He had a hold on me mentally and sexually. I can admit I was a big dummy. I was just looking for attention from a man because I didn't have it growing up from my father. My dad was in and out of jail for various reasons, and I would look for any amount of attention from men to compensate and fill the hole in my heart. I remember there was one incident when *Mr. MIA* and his friend and I went to the M&M Mart on Angier Ave. I got out of the car and asked if they wanted anything from the store. Boy, why did I do that? When *Mr. MIA* and I entered the store, he let me have it! He quickly became jealous and got angry with me for simply asking what his friend wanted, implying that my basic consideration of him was somehow flirtatious. He then made distasteful, lewd comments about me. Everybody in the store looked at me in total shock. Feeling embarrassed, I quickly left. I was trying to be nice, but he wasn't having it. I was silent the entire way back to his crib. After about a couple of months, he went missing. That's why I gave him the name *Mr. MIA*. At the time, I had no clue what happened to him. I took that as my way out. I didn't hear from him for months. However, one day, I decided to buy the slammer, a publication that listed all the people who were locked up for various crimes in the city. I was skimming through to see if I noticed anyone, and lo and behold, I see *Mr. MIA*! He was locked up for kidnapping and assault with a deadly weapon. What in the world had my life come to? At that moment, I felt God spared me. I don't know what happened and didn't care to know at that point.

Nevertheless, I found out I was nine weeks and one day pregnant with his child. He never knew until the day I ran into him. Of course, he denied it, but I knew for a fact it was his. I took the calendar and traced back to the exact day my child was conceived, which was the day we had intercourse. My stomach hit the floor. What was I supposed to do? I hadn't graduated college yet, and I knew for a fact I was in no shape to bring a child into this world. So, I called on my Aunt T. We had a family discussion, and we all decided it was wise to take a trip to the local Planned Parenthood facility. We all know what happens there. As I entered, I noticed some familiar faces, a few ladies who attended school with me. I will keep their identities hidden. This was an experience I never want to go through again. I wouldn't wish this on my worst enemy. Yep, you guessed it. I had an abortion. It is nothing that I'm proud of, but at the time I thought it was necessary.

There wasn't any way I was getting ready to bring a kid into this world, and I was in an impoverished condition. I could barely take care of myself, and to think about taking care of a kid. Nope, it seemed impossible! I promised God if He forgave me and gave me another opportunity to have another kid, I would not abort it. Lo and behold, a year later my second child was conceived (talk about not learning the lesson and repeating the same cycle). You better know I kept my promise with God. My beautiful son was born at 9 lbs. and 9 oz.! I cherish him every day.

However, at the time, what should have been a celebratory moment, was a funeral in my eyes. You would think that a mother would be happy when her child was born. But not me. I had met his dad through an online site. We clicked, and the rest was history. I applied for Section 8, got me a place, and we moved in together. Life was sweet until he told me he couldn't have kids. I believed him (like a fool). He said he had tried having kids before but wasn't successful. I wasn't happy at all. To find out I was a mom, it was heartbreaking to say the least. My life seemed to stop all of a sudden, to think I fell for his deception. I had to deal with mental incapability's on top of being a new mother.

There were times I didn't want to even look at my baby. I didn't want to change his diaper or bathe him. When I delivered him by emergency C-section, the doctor tried to hand him to me, and I refused. He was covered in blood and stuff. I didn't want that all over me. Nope! That's when I knew I had it bad. For most first-time moms, that's a time to bond with your kid.

I didn't have that experience. I'm glad I had supportive family and friends at the time, who knew about what I was experiencing and recommended I see a professional. So, I did. Besides my child's father, I had an aunt who came to help out with the baby. As far as I can remember, I took medications for a couple of months and thought I didn't need them anymore. They made me feel like a walking zombie. I didn't like how they made me feel, so I stopped taking them.

Then, our relationship took a turn for the worst. We started having significant issues. I felt he was negatively influencing me. I felt I was losing myself. To feel accepted, I imitated him and did what he did. After a while, I noticed something was off. He would be acting weird or he couldn't go to sleep. I later found out he was using cocaine, and I became curious. I tried it; it was euphoric. I liked it, and after a while I started using regularly with him, mainly as a sex drug. I'll go more in depth in the *White Girl* chapter.

Many in our community were doing it too, so I thought it wasn't a big deal. I told my dad and mom about my habit. My dad educated me about it. At that time, he was in the game. He told me the dangers, what to do and what not to do, what to look for when buying it, etc. One thing I can say is I never did it outside of the house or around people who didn't do it.

I always made sure to never put it before my kid or my bills. I thought I had a good system going. No one knew for years, not even my neighbors. However, I had an *ah-ha* moment. I didn't stay on it for long. I realized I had to pull myself up by my bootstraps. I had to make up my mind I wanted better for myself and my kid. I was on and off with my child's father for eleven years. I had slip-ups from time to time, but I got through it. Being with him, I endured a lot. I guess that's what made me so strong. I witnessed him attempt suicide at least six times, be homeless, and be an alcoholic. He had a hard life, and I guess that was his way of coping. I tried seeking help for him, but I still found myself always running back to him in the process. I don't know. I guess I had this thing inside of me that just wanted to help people. How in the world was I supposed to help others when I couldn't help myself? I just felt it was something missing. I loved the bad guys, and I was drawn to them. Despite what this man did or didn't do, however, I *can* say that he took care of my child financially. He may not have been there as much as I liked, but I was grateful for the time and money he did give. I will forever admire that about him.

# CHAPTER 2
## WHITE GIRL

This chapter was hard for me to write. I may face some backlash from my family and peers, but I have to speak it. It's my truth and I would rather tell it myself than give the power away to someone else. It will entail all the juicy details of how I was introduced to her, the type of relationship I formed with her, and how I ended up divorcing her. At the time, I was in a relationship for many years, and I always said I would never be *that girl*. Taking a peek in the rearview mirror, I realized I have always been around the *white girl*. I was exposed to her at a very young age, so it was nothing to me. Many of you are thinking, "Who is this white girl?" It isn't what you think. The phrase I'm referring to describes a drug. Today's generation calls it *nose candy*. Am I embarrassed to come out and expose who I used to be? Absolutely not! I just pray that this testimony will help free someone of that stronghold.

It all started with being exposed to it through a family member. They were dealing on the street, and I used to be around when they bagged it and sold it. That was normal to me. I have always told myself I wouldn't become a product of my environment, but I did anyway. Life got in the way.

Let's fast forward a bit. I never touched this drug in my younger days, but the day I did, I was in a relationship with someone.

Let me explain. In the Bible, God tells us we are made in His image. Well, take that principle and apply it to whom you're dating. That's what happened to me. I was the spitting image of this man. I loved him dearly. Because of that, I indulged in many things he did just to feel close to him. I changed myself for him. I know it's stupid, but at the time it made sense. Love is blind. and it will make you do things you wouldn't normally do. I accepted him for who he was. I knew he also dabbled in that drug along with drinking. It didn't bother me at first, but as time went by his behavior got irrational. One night, we were in the bedroom, and he decided to get him a bag or two. As he was doing his thing, I had the urge to do it too. Up until this point, I had never done this drug. He didn't stop me, but why did I expect him to. I should've stopped myself. So, I did it. I didn't feel anything at first. Then it hit me all at once, a high like I had never felt. It was like my body was possessed. I couldn't stop. It heightened my sex drive. We indulged all night. This went off and on for a couple of years, undetected from those around me, but one day I decided to let my parents know. I thought I'd tell them rather than have someone in the streets do it first. Although I only purchased from one guy, no one knew. They took it better than I thought they would. My dad said, "Well, if you're going to do it, these are the do's and don'ts." He educated me on it. Most parents would be ready to disown their own child, but not mine. I guess you can say I have forgiving parents, and I'm grateful for that. My father just didn't seem to care. And my mother, while she had her reservations about it, didn't care to discuss the situation with me. I think she was too embarrassed.

So, life went on. I was a normal, functioning person living with this secret, only my parents knew. It became my normal. However, I always tried my best not to let my habits affect my relationship with my son and my duty to him. Most people I knew just didn't care.

But after a while, I grew tired of doing it. I burned myself out.

Something clicked inside me. I decided I wanted better for myself. I don't know what happened, but after going through postpartum depression and being diagnosed with situational bipolar disorder, I knew I wanted better. I expressed that to my lover at the time, but I knew he was too far gone. That's when our souls began to split slowly. I tried to wean myself off of the drug cold turkey. Every now and then, I would dabble in it, but I would feel terrible afterwards. I needed help at that point, and that's when I began to call on God. I wanted more for myself. I had a whole life to think about, and I knew I had to make a change. I decided to try to move on from the relationship by keeping myself busy. There is a reason the front windshield of a car is bigger than the rear!

# CHAPTER 3
## PRO-CHOICE

After having an abortion, this is the first verse of a song I wrote. This song helped me deal with the worst decision of my life.

**Verse :1** *"I'm not anti, I'm pro-choice. I wasn't forced to do what I did or do what I'm gonna do, so if you haven't had the experience then I ain't talking to you. Listen up, all of you. That abortion had me lost, and I was all caught in the rapture of emotions. The situation was crazy for real. See, I didn't even wanna go half on his baby, especially not by a criminal. It's critical. I'd rather be depressed and drink five bottles of Pinnacle. I had to make up my mind. I was on the way to the clinic, got tears in my eyes. Have mercy on my soul, Lord. Don't blame me because I'm pro-choice. Thank God he gave me a voice to speak and help those in remorse. Just need my place in heaven so Lord, just forgive me!"*

**Hook:** *This is a message to you. I'm going through this with you. I feel the pain that you do. This is my story. I know there are brighter days. After we move past the rain, know that we all feel the same. This is our story!*

**Verse 2:** *I checked in and patiently waited, looking around noticing everyone with sad faces. The nurse called me up, then it was my turn. I never looked back, moving forward was my concern. The doctor asked me if I wanted an ultrasound. I said, "YES, so I can at least see my child." The baby waved goodbye. That was wild. I ain't ever gonna forget that last moment. Off to the next room I went. I was very curious of what the next procedure entailed. Scared, but I knew I had to finish it. I hadn't done that before, so I said to myself, "Not ever, no more. This s\*\*\* is real. In my mind, body, and spirit, I feel the disconnection of affection. Best believe, I learned my lesson. If I ever get pregnant again, it would be a blessing."*

That was an outward expression of the many emotions I felt at the time. I can vividly remember that day, and I will never forget it. This chapter is dedicated to my unborn child, who I decided to terminate. Earlier in the book, I mentioned Mr. MIA. He stood in my face and told me the child couldn't be his. How dare he since he knew I wasn't with anyone else. The aborted child was his. I sometimes regret it, but I have come to terms and asked God to forgive me. However, looking back I realized I made that decision out of hurt and anger. I pray that God has forgiven me and washed that blood off of my hands before I stand at the pearly gates.

The second verse of the song walked you through every moment of the process. From checking in at the front desk, to the actual abortion procedure, to the after-effects. I don't wish that trauma on my worst enemy. God knows and sees everything that we do, and He wouldn't put more on us than we can bear. Something deep down in my spirit told me not to have that abortion, but because the guy left me, I was angry and hurt and didn't want to raise a child alone. Also, I had outside influences that convinced me that I wasn't ready, like my mom and aunts. Of course, people always have a lot to say when it isn't their responsibility.

Awhile afterwards, I got on my knees and asked God for forgiveness and I repented. I am not opposed to people having a choice to have an abortion, but if you follow Christ, you know it is against his commandment - Thou shall not kill. God gives us free will, and it is up to us to make the right choice. I have since moved on from that incident and forgiven myself. One year later, I conceived a baby boy! I knew then I was meant to be a mother. To God be the Glory!

# CHAPTER 4
## KEEPING UP WITH
## THE JONESES

I am the only child of both parents. For me, family is important. My family was well known in our city. We were known to gamble, play cards, have parties, drink, and hang out with each other every chance we got. We liked to have fun! Till this day, we still hang out at each other's houses just to sing karaoke, crack jokes, and enjoy each other's company. Growing up, all I could remember was having a house full of people every weekend. You know everybody has that one family member's house that they go over to every day to eat or every weekend to trip out! My mom had the go-to house for years. Even the neighborhood thugs used to stop by and make sure she was okay. You can bet that every weekend we had folks in and out on a consistent basis. She hardly kept any food because she was the type of person that wanted to make sure everyone ate and had a good meal. I used to think that my mom never had time for me because she was too busy entertaining her guests. I guess people loved her personality, and she got along with everybody. If you were hungry, she fed you, or if you needed a beer my mom made sure you had one. I looked forward to those days — everybody sitting around getting drunk and playing tunk, spades, and 5000. My family loved gambling. It was in their blood. I did it for fun because it was all I knew, but it wasn't a sport so to speak. My mom's favorite game was Pokeno. It was like a Bingo game, but the board was made up of playing cards, and each round you had to put up quarters, nickels, or dimes in about five cups. Now, just imagine how much money you could win. Those habits came from my grandparents. My grandmother used to drink alcohol back in her day before she got saved, and my granddad used to be in North Durham playing the tip boards and picking numbers; drinking was a hobby for him as well.

Some of my family was born and raised in Connecticut, New Haven. Some stayed but my grandmother moved down south to Durham. Eventually, she went blind. I couldn't imagine losing my eyesight and having to count on the people around me for everything. She didn't lose hope though. My grandmother accepted who she was and learned to adapt to a different lifestyle. You wouldn't even know she was blind if she didn't tell you. Man, listen. That lady can cook you under the table! She arranged her furniture to make pathways for her to walk. She folded her money so she could recognize what she had. She learned how to read and write Braille and learned how to make pottery. I still remember the whooping she gave me. It was so funny, and I laugh at it now because I didn't understand the power she commanded. Let me tell you! That was the worst spanking I had in my life. How can I not out-run a person who is blind? One day, it was me and my cousin in the kitchen at Grandma's house. We began to argue over my coat because my cousin had been stepping on it. I loved my coat and wasn't pleased that she was soiling it for no reason. You know, back in the day when one got a whooping, everybody got a whooping. The older folks didn't leave nobody out. No one was safe! I was mad as a firecracker! All I remember was grandma chasing me around that house like we were running track at the Olympics. I thought to myself, "How in the world is she able to catch me if she can't see?" When Grandma got a hold of me.....I'm going to leave your imagination there.

As for my granddad, may he rest in peace. Pops used to get under my skin so bad (in a good way of course). I used to go to Grandma's after coming home from school and used to have to watch Matlock, Gilligan's Island, and the westerns. Man, there were times where I'd be sitting in front of the tv hoping it wouldn't get a signal from the antenna. They had one of those televisions with the knobs and one was always missing. We sometimes had to take pliers to turn it. I used to dislike going to Grandma's, but it was also the most liberating at times. Hearing those old stories, getting wiped down with holy oil and blue magic hair grease, and eating homemade biscuits... ain't nothing like that good ole wisdom and learning life lessons.

I was that child that aggravated everybody. I used to do it on purpose too. For instance, we all had the same amount of food. I didn't care if it was a snack. I would purposely wait until everybody ate their food, then eat mine. I used to eat it slowly too. My cousins used to be so mad. They would knock my food out of my hand because it made them hungry. But I love my family. Family is everything. We have our ups and downs, fights, agreements and disagreements. Best believe though if anybody comes for any one of us, we will have each other's back! Remember, we don't have to keep up with the Joneses, WE *ARE* THE JONESES!

# CHAPTER 5
## MARRIED TO THE GAME!

Just what it says, I was married to the game. What game? Messing with a married man. I didn't want to admit it at the time when I was in my mess. Yep, some of you reading this may be shocked because you can't imagine a person like me, a person who had stuff going for herself, a person who seemed to have it all together, would be messing with a married man. Yep, you guessed it, and I'm not proud of it either. Not one bit! I have to be transparent, though; it felt good to do it at the time. Let me start by saying, vengeance was mine, or so I thought. It all started with the "other woman." Little did I know, *I* was the other woman. I also realized that one of the reasons I allowed such a thing to happen because I was harboring jealousy and envy deep within my heart. I didn't recognize this at the time, but I wanted to be married desperately, not even fully understanding marriage. I just wanted what she had, so I did anything necessary to fill that void. I got a thrill out of having multiple rendezvous and coming to family functions only to fantasize about the what ifs. It was amazing to share intimate moments every chance we got. I admit I knew that it was wrong to do. What is a girl supposed to do when she felt like this person came in and took what was rightfully hers? I was on and off with this guy, so in my mind, we were still together. His actions displayed he was in it for the long haul, to look up one day and now he's married. Oh no, no, no! I was overseas in St. Martin on vacation when I heard the news. You better believe that ignited the fire within me. I was a woman scorned, one mad black woman! Quite naturally, women protect what's theirs Let's talk about Tyler Perry's *A Diary of a Mad Black Woman.* I wasn't mad, I was livid!

I just didn't care. At this time, it was a game to me. I figured he was mine, and again I sought revenge! It came back to bite me in the behind. BIG TIME! This man had a way with words that could convince anybody. I had intelligence but was lacking that street knowledge. As folks would say, I had a whole lot of book sense but no common sense. I guess common sense isn't so common. I was a nerd, so that street life wasn't second nature to me. A part of me wanted him to leave his wife, so I told him things to try to get him to change his mind. It almost happened, but deep down inside I didn't want a full-time relationship with him. I'm not ashamed to say that there's some deep-rooted issues when a person does such a thing. It takes growth, deliverance, and a whole lot of self-reflection to fix that kind of brokenness. However, let us not forget that it takes two to engage in adultery. Often, it's the woman who takes the blame, as if it's all her fault that the man stepped out, and that's not the case. You can't just blame the woman. Yes, she is supposed to be wise enough not to entertain the thought, but the bigger issue at hand is why is the man even thinking about going outside the marriage? This went on for some time until I decided I deserved more. I had to get on my knees and ask God to forgive me of my sins and cleanse my heart of anger, rejection, bitterness, and ask Him to break the soul-tie that was present. Once I did this, the Holy Spirit told me to apologize to his wife. This was hard to do–knowingly being a part of the problem that caused infidelity. I reached out to her through Facebook and asked for her forgiveness. I offered her to accompany me to lunch to talk about it, as grown women ought to do. Of course, she denied it and was not ready to face the truth. How could I blame her? I surely wouldn't want to sit across the table from a woman who wouldn't leave my man alone. It would go down on-site if you ask me! But I knew she and I had to heal, and that's cool. I admitted my faults and confessed my sins to her and asked for her forgiveness. Whether she accepted it or not, my hands were washed of that blood. I laid everything at the altar. It took months to really get over him and the situation. I thank God for deliverance. Jesus is real! I didn't want that karma, and I wouldn't wish that experience on my worst enemy. I don't know what would possess a woman into thinking that you can prevent a man from leaving you. If he isn't invested emotionally or spiritually, he won't stay. Not even having a baby will make him stay, sis. So, let that man go to where he wants to be. Trust me, the majority of the time the grass is never greener! He will try and claw his way back once he realizes he messed up. But you be strong and continue to look forward. Have tunnel vision and don't allow distractions or the enemy's voice to deceive you into going back to what had you bound.

# CHAPTER 6
## GOD'S GRACE IS SUFFICIENT!

How many people know that in your low moments, God's grace is sufficient? I can raise several hands on that one. Sometimes when we are in the wilderness, we can't feel or see Him, but we must know He is always there, guiding our footsteps in the way we should go. In this chapter, I pray you will take a nugget that can help you on your journey. Let's be selfless and help someone else.

In 2017, I was still on Section 8 housing, receiving Medicaid, food stamps, and I sometimes got a welfare check. Me and my son were living in a two-bedroom house. Bills started rolling in, and I started to wonder why my light bill and water bill were extremely high every month. So I did what anyone else would have done. I called the City of Durham's Neighborhood services and notified my caseworker.

They launched an inspection, and lo and behold they found ten violations. My landlord had thirty days to fix these issues, but of course she didn't, and they told me I had two weeks to move out. In shock, I panicked. Where in the world would I find some place to stay in two weeks on section 8? I tried to port my voucher over to Wake county. Their process was much quicker than Durham's, and I was in a relocation class within one week. Then, I went through that process to get approved for an apartment. The unthinkable happened. I received a call by the caseworker of Wake County, and she told me some devastating news. She said, "Ms. Jones, I regret having to tell you that you do not qualify for our Section 8 program." I was baffled at that point because I had just gotten approved for an apartment, and she was telling me I made too much money to be on the program. Now, most people would have been mad, but I was just confused at what was going on. She said she could port my voucher back over to Durham Housing Authority. I thanked her for helping me as much as she could and hung up the phone. Another week went by before I got a call from Mrs. G. I remember it like it was yesterday. I was sitting in the parking lot of Walmart in Morrisville when I got the call. Mrs. G told me to brace myself. It was weird because I felt a sense of peace come over me. What she told me next would change the trajectory of my future. She said, "Take this as a blessing in disguise. God will not bring you out if He wasn't going to bless you. It will be hard, but I know you were chosen to withstand what's coming next." That lady told me that I was denied. She told me I made too much money! I was getting denied again and this time in Durham! I went through so many emotions, it was ridiculous. At the time, I didn't know what to do. My credit was jacked up, and I didn't know what my next move was. So, there I was with no place to stay. I had to swallow my pride and contact my mom to tell her what was happening. She offered to keep my son with her but didn't offer me the same until a later time. She took my son in, and I was hurt, but I knew Christ Jesus would strengthen me.

I was homeless for about a month. No one knew, but I would take wash-ups in the storage unit complex bathroom twice a day. I would change clothes in my storage unit, take naps, etc. I continued my daily life of going to work, church, and everything. No one knew...so I thought. One day, my old Apostle came to me after church and asked me what was wrong. I told her nothing, but somehow she knew. She said to me, "I've noticed that your hair hasn't been kept up. You're not dressing the way you used to, and I don't see your son as often with you anymore. She looked right through to my soul with those eyes, and I began to weep uncontrollably. Apostle knew then that I wasn't okay. I had to tell her what was going on, so she called on a member of the church and asked if I was able to stay with them until I got on my feet. The member said yes and gave me three months to get myself together (this was around June, July, and August of 2017). Within three months, I found an apartment around the corner and moved in that September. To God be the Glory. All of this was for my making. I just had to trust God to make a way and He did. As you know, for every new level, there's a new adversary or obstacle to overcome. Not even a month after I moved in, I believe God put me through another test.

Since I knew what it felt like to be homeless and down on my luck, I had a friend who needed help. I told her that she could crash with me. I couldn't bear the thought of knowing my friend was going through a similar situation. I thanked God for blessing me so I could bless someone else. Talk about coming full circle. I am telling you all this not to boast, but for you to know my heart posture.

So, let's fast forward. I was at my son's football game talking with some of the moms about home ownership and how I wanted to give my son a better life than I had growing up. The coach overheard me and decided to set aside some time to talk. When we did, he revealed to me that he was a millionaire, owning an airplane school out in Fort Bragg and had a home he was looking to rent out. That sounded good to me and I thought about it. I was excited. I knew God sent that man with that opportunity. I said to myself, *If I'm paying about $1000 a month for a two-bedroom apartment (including lights, water, etc.), surely I can afford this!* I didn't know one of the football moms was a social worker for the self-sufficiency program at DSS, and she said to me, "Your name sounds so familiar!" About a week went by and she told me I needed to come and see her because I may have some money that was waiting to be claimed. I was doubtful, but I'm all about them coins so without hesitation I made my way down there. Lo and behold, I had saved over $12,000 in an escrow account. I had completed all of the terms of agreement and a check was cut immediately. There was my chance to give my son a better life! I moved in December of 2017 to a five-bedroom home in a community that was gorgeous! It was gated with security, had seven lakes, a pier, swimming pool, golf course, basketball court, an exercise trail, baseball field, farmers market, etc. I could not believe my eyes! *How could God bless me like this? What did I do to deserve this? My God, thank you, Father.* The story soon turned......I hadn't been in the house a good six months before my paradise was shaken. I was working a good paying job at the cable company in Morrisville, NC. I was one of the top saleswomen on my team. I was there for about one year and four months. Then, the unthinkable happened. I began having issues with my babysitter. She wasn't able to continue to take care of my kid anymore. I understood it wasn't her responsibility or her fault, but it was just wrong timing in my opinion. So, I went to my supervisor, then their manager, and then all the way to the HR Director. To my surprise, they helped as much as they could. I used up my two weeks of PTO time to try and see if I could work something out. Unfortunately, I couldn't, and I was hurt because I knew what I was going to have to do next. I ended up giving my two weeks' notice to the HR Director. I left in good standing, but I was at the lowest moment of my life! That was in April of 2018. What was I supposed to do? Here I am in this big ole house and didn't know how I was supposed to pay for it. In that same month, I got into a hit-and-run accident. I got my car fixed but couldn't find another job for months, which put me behind on car payments and rent. (Mind you, I'm in a seller's financing agreement, so I'm renting to own my home).

I began hiding my car from the repo man, and I was afraid to contact my landlord and tell him I could no longer afford my home. Everyone knows when you break your lease, you are still responsible for the remainder of the contract. But man, does God provide! My landlord then told me, "No biggie, I understand you are trying to escape poverty and want a better life for your kid. I'll work with you." That was the hardest I prayed in a long time. My landlord allowed me to stay in the house for six months without paying a dime! All I had to do was tag a little extra money onto the rent every month to help pay off what I owed. God's grace is sufficient! I was granted a blessing I know came from God himself. I couldn't survive without Him.

Finally, I let the repo man take the car because I could no longer afford it anyway. I even started having dreams of the car being taken, so I knew that was God communicating with me to let it go. I know now that God can't replace something if that something is still in the way. Fortunately, my mom told me I could drive her car until I got back on my feet. Let's talk about *favor*. As I said before, there is always one thing after another. What the devil fails to do at one time in your life, he tries to do it again later. In the midst of those trials, God always had something new to teach me to strengthen my faith.

It's now 2019, and my faith is being stretched like never before. I can't begin to tell you all how I am still living in this beautiful home, making ends meet. There were times, even after all my hardships with the rent and the car, I had to go to the food shelter because we couldn't afford groceries. My son's school also had this program where they would send food home on the weekends, which I was also thankful for. Let's talk about having to eat a slice of humble pie! I even had people tell me I couldn't afford the house, and I needed to move back in with my mom. Despite what other's said, I continued to push through and trusted God. I had faith in his promises for my life, so I didn't pay no mind to other's advice or opinions. I am not ashamed to tell you my story. I tell it to help you understand that your *now* isn't your future! Learn the lesson and continue to push forward. God will provide when the time is right. Surely, He will reveal Himself. A promise is still a promise!

# CHAPTER 7
## LOSING MY RELIGION

I know most of you are thinking this chapter will be about bashing the modern-day church, but it's not. It's not about who's religion is the right one or what your beliefs are. This chapter is about my journey in seeking to find Christ. It's messy at times, but it is raw, honest, and true.

I have a memory of when I was around 18 years old. I was invited to a church service at Grace Church of Durham up on Cornwallis Road in Durham, NC. I had no idea what was in store for me that day, but I encountered something I didn't recognize. The preacher preached so good that my feet began to move uncontrollably. As church folks would say, "My feet got to shuffling." I couldn't stop praising the Lord through shouting. It was a feeling I can't explain; I was fully conscious in my mind but had no physical control over my body. Something had taken over me. People in the church told me I was shouting non-stop for 15 minutes or more. To me, it felt like five minutes. I felt so good after calming my spirit. I could feel the weight lifted off of me. That experience scared the living hell out of me. Literally! I had no clue what or who had taken over my body, but I knew that I didn't want it to happen again. Not having control over what you think belongs to you is scary. I knew nothing about the Holy Spirit then, but I promised myself I wasn't going back to church. For years I didn't attend, but little did I know God had other plans.

In the meantime, I was in hair school, and I was introduced to the Muslim community by a friend of mine. She didn't force anything on me, but I wanted to learn more about the Koran and the language they spoke. I'm not going to lie; I was intrigued by some of her morals and values. She taught me about the culture of their men and women, why they had to pray five times a day, why they had to cover themselves, etc. I was very curious. I thought a lot of their principles made sense. Still, I was looking for much more. I knew there had to be more than what I was being exposed to.

Fast forward, in college I had a dorm mate who was a Seventh Day Adventist. I also dated a guy who was studying to be a Jehovah's Witness, and I had friends who studied the teachings of Kemet. I have been exposed to most religions that exist. They all influenced me and taught me something in some way. However, none of them felt right. Yes, maybe I found useful ways to live and do good, but I still felt empty, and I wanted to be whole. However, nothing came close to Christianity.

Fast forward to 2013. I was working at a local hair shop. When the owner and I began to talk about the things of God, she asked me if I had a church home. I told her no, and she consequently invited me to her church. I kindly accepted the invitation. It only took me two visits before I became a member. Not long after that, I was put to work! I sat under the head videographer for about six months and learned everything I needed to know. Next thing I knew, I was now running it all by myself – recording, editing, duplicating, and sending the tape off to the local TV station. I did this for about four years until another assignment was given to me. I became Church administrator. Talk about responsibility! However, I was up for the challenge. Here I was in my fifth year of being a member, and I started to question why I wasn't truly feeling elevated in the natural or in the spirit. After attending some Saturday classes, going to multiple Bible study sessions, and attending conferences, I still felt I wasn't growing. I am not sure if I was being overlooked, acting out of my flesh, or if it was God inadvertently telling me I had outgrown where I was spiritually. Either way, I thirsted for something more. I wanted to feel close to God and have a true spiritual experience rather than just go through the motions. I began to think maybe it wasn't meant for me to be a minister, prophet, or an evangelist. Maybe I was supposed to just operate the camera. Just when I was about to crawl back into my shell, the unthinkable started to happen. I was told by a well-known pastor, "It is time to come from behind the camera." The prophet came to warn, edify, and confirm the Word of God. That is exactly what happened. First the pastor, then the prophet, and lastly another pastor came to tell me the exact same thing. All in all, this message came about five times over the course of a year. I couldn't ignore the call anymore. I knew in my spirit I had outgrown my current place of worship. It was time for me to leave.

Then, fear took hold of me. I was afraid to tell my leader. I went into prayer and asked a friend to do the same. Months passed, and I finally got the strength to write a letter. That Sunday, I was prepared to give the letter to my leader, but I couldn't do it. Not that it wasn't meant for me to do so, but I didn't have enough courage. I knew how Jesus felt when he began to weep. I was crying a river that day. Talk about being in bondage! Some people (myself included) don't know that they are in bondage until they are out. The Sunday after that, I had a deliverance session and when I came out of it, I looked at my leader and let everything out! It hurt me to say it, but I did so anyway. I felt so free afterwards, like I was delivered from that Jezebel spirit.

This event in my life was difficult, but it led me to know I was making the right decision. I felt the release of control and the hold of the spirit that held me captive. I know people have been hurt by some of the things folks have done to them while in the church, but the church is not God. It's just a building where you go to partake in fellowship, listen to His Word, and worship. Instead of telling others you experienced church hurt, take the time to read Matthew 18:15-17. You will then gain more understanding. Sometimes people judge or insinuate too much. They think they know you when they don't. People don't go to church to get embarrassed. They go to get healing and guidance. Although conviction and rebuke play a necessary role, we must show mercy and cover our brothers and sisters in Christ with love above all. However, if you don't receive that from your church home, it must not distort your perception of Christ. Unfortunately, I learned that lesson the hard way.

I left the church. That's when I began to literally lose my religion! I was hurt and confused but separating myself from the house of God was not the answer. All of the things I thought I knew, I had to unlearn and relearn God's way. I do understand that order have to be set in the house of God, but when it interferes with what God is telling you to do for Him, this is where the problem lies. If God has his own rules and principles for us to live by, why in the world do we [church folks] make up our own? The flesh and heart are misleading, and God tells us in His word that we should "Study to show thyself approved unto God, a workman that needeth not to be ashamed, rightly dividing the word of truth" (2 Timothy 2:15 KJV).

We go to church to be fed the word and to fellowship with our brethren. Majority of the time, the sermons that come across the pulpit are based on the personal experiences of the person preaching.

However, I have had several experiences throughout my journey where I knew what was being taught wasn't the truth! It was their truth but not God's truth. We must be careful to discern truth from fiction and adhere to God's word when what we hear doesn't align with the scriptures. Likewise, if we are able to preach, we must be vigilant and pray to God for wisdom in guiding and influencing a large group of people, being careful not to lead them astray.

After church that day, I went outside. I looked up in the sky, and there was an eagle circling around the top of the building. I believe that was God's way of telling me I made the right decision. Some say eagles are symbols of a prophet. The eagle represents supremacy. It reigns as the chief over the bird kingdom. It dominates its territory. When a storm hits, eagles fly above it and through it. Eagles are also visionaries. They see their prey, they plan their course of attack, and then they take action at the right time. Like God, the eagle flies high and sees low.

Ever since that day, I have flourished in the spirit. I have learned so much about God. My praise is different, my heavenly language has changed, and most importantly, my faith has gotten stronger! My current church home is wonderful, and I thank God for my brothers and sisters there. The people are genuine, and we are all striving for the same thing – to have an up-close experience with God. It is truly an unconventional non-denominational church. They allow the Holy Spirit to lead the service. They are not worried about a time frame, a program to follow, etc. God truly has his way in that place and through the people. I encourage everyone to seek God and ask for instructions and clarity about what to do when hardships arise.

I believe God delivered me out of bondage. For that, I'm thankful. I sit under leaders who know no boundaries, only freedom! They taught me how to rightfully divide the word of God and to test the spirits by the spirit. They teach how to apply biblical principles and don't just instruct you to write notes and study. I remember my first month there. The apostle of the church told me in front of everybody, "The reason I had you sit down and not do anything is because God told me you are overworked." God wanted me to focus on building my relationship with Him. I hadn't had the chance to sit and learn because I was always working in the previous church. I knew then they weren't trying to pimp my gifts for the sake of benefiting the church. I will not allow myself to follow man. Instead, I've learned to follow God. This has been an awesome journey. I've been in the valley and as low as the pits. There is nowhere to go but up from here. I am grateful to have experienced the highs and lows in my life, as well as my journey to walking with Christ. Ultimately, we go through things in order to help the next person overcome their battles. I pray that those reading my story will also be graced for impact!

www.ingramcontent.com/pod-product-compliance
Lightning Source LLC
Chambersburg PA
CBHW031528040426
42445CB00009B/443